First World War
and Army of Occupation
War Diary
France, Belgium and Germany

41 DIVISION
123 Infantry Brigade
Queen's (Royal West Surrey Regiment)
2/4th Battalion
1 March 1919 - 30 September 1919

WO95/2638/2

The Naval & Military Press Ltd
www.nmarchive.com
Published in association with The National Archives

Published by

The Naval & Military Press Ltd

Unit 10 Ridgewood Industrial Park,

Uckfield, East Sussex,

TN22 5QE England

Tel: +44 (0) 1825 749494

www.naval-military-press.com

www.nmarchive.com

This diary has been reprinted in facsimile from the original. Any imperfections are inevitably reproduced and the quality may fall short of modern type and cartographic standards.

© Crown Copyright
Images reproduced by permission of The National Archives, London, England, 2015.

Contents

Document type	Place/Title	Date From	Date To
Heading	WO95/2638/3 2/4 Queen's (R.W Surrey) Mar 19-Sept 19		
Heading	2/4 Bn Q.R. West Surreys 1919 Mar-Sep 1919		
War Diary	Wahn	01/03/1919	01/03/1919
War Diary	Engelskirchen	28/03/1919	28/03/1919
War Diary		01/04/1919	30/04/1919
War Diary	Ehreshoven	01/05/1919	26/05/1919
War Diary	Lindlar	28/05/1919	28/05/1919
Miscellaneous Operation(al) Order(s)	2/4th Battalion The Queens Regiment Order No. 2	27/05/1919	27/05/1919
Miscellaneous	Defence Scheme For The Left Battalion (Lindlar Section) Reference Map 3 S. S.E.		
War Diary	Lindlar	01/06/1919	30/06/1919
Miscellaneous	Names Of Officers Leaving The Battalion During Month Of June	01/07/1919	01/07/1919
War Diary	Lindlarm	01/07/1919	31/07/1919
War Diary	Frankenforst	01/08/1919	30/08/1919
Miscellaneous	War Diary 2nd London L. T. M. Coy.	01/08/1919	01/08/1919
War Diary	Haus Frankenforst	01/09/1919	24/09/1919
Operation(al) Order(s)	2/4th. Battalion "The Queens" Regt. Operation Order No.1	22/09/1919	22/09/1919
Operation(al) Order(s)	2/4th. Battalion "The Queens" Regt. Operation Order No. 2	23/09/1919	23/09/1919
War Diary		01/09/1919	30/09/1919

WO95/2638 ③
2/4 Queen's (R.W.Surrey)
Mar'19 – Sept'19

LONDON DIVISION
(LATE 41ST DIVISION)
123RD INFY BDE

2/4 ~~4~~TH BN Q.R.WEST SURREYS
1919 MAR - SEP 1919

FROM 34 DIV
101 Bde

WAR DIARY or INTELLIGENCE SUMMARY

PLACE and DATE	
WAHN. 1.3.19	The Battalion remained in WAHN barracks until March 3, 1919. On March 3, the Bn. moved by march route to KALK and were billeted from the 101 Bde. 34th London Division & the 123 Bn. 4th London Division. The Battalion was to Divisional reserve and general training specially ceremonial was carried out. The Battalion remained at KALK until March 28, at which date it took over the outposts in the ENGELSKIRCHEN area, finding 7 outed posts with 2 companies and 2 companies in reserve.
ENGELSKIRCHEN. 28.3.19.	**Strength.** During the month the strength of the Battalion has been decreased by 3 officers and 48. O.R. and increased by 4 officers and 461. O.R. **Health.** **Food:** average sickness 2%. **Weather** Generally mild with considerable rainfall.

Wm Hill
Lt Colonel
Commanding
"6th The Queens"

Army Form C. 2118.

WAR DIARY
or
INTELLIGENCE SUMMARY.
(Erase heading not required.)

Instructions regarding War Diaries and Intelligence Summaries are contained in F. S. Regs., Part II. and the Staff Manual respectively. Title pages will be prepared in manuscript.

Place	Date	Hour	Summary of Events and Information	Remarks and references to Appendices
	April 1st. 1919.		During the whole month this Battalion was quartered in the ENGELSKIRCHEN area, with 2 Companies in the outpost, 1 in support, and 1 in reserve. The right Company at HARDT and FELKLESBURG. The left Company at BLUMENAU and ROMMERSBURG. and Battalion Headquarters and support and reserve Companies in the ENGELSKIRCHEN area. General training, including firing on the 30 yds range, was carried out throughout the month.	
	April 7th. 1919.		On April 7th. 1919 General Sir H.C.O. Plumer. G.C.B. G.C.M.G. G.C.V.O. A.D.C. Commanding the Army of the Rhine presented the Battalion with the Union Flag on behalf of His Majesty the King.	
	April 9th. 1919.		On April 9th. 1919 Lieut. Colonel S.T. WATSON. D.S.O. The Queen's Regt. assumed Command of the Battalion, vice Lieut. Colonel. W.J.M. HILL. DSO. Scots Guards, to England, demobilised.	
	April 11th. 1919.		On April 11th. 1919 The 53rd. Young Soldiers Battalion, The Queen's Regiment joined this Battalion and was absorbed into the strength of 2/4th. Battalion. The Queen's Regiment.	
	April 30th. 1919.		On April 30th. 1919, the Battalion was relieved in the outposts by 11th. The Queen's Regiment and took over from 10th. Battalion. The Queen's Regiment in Brigade reserve in the EHRESHOVEN area, with 2 Companies at LOOPE, 1 Company at BUSSENBACH, and 1 Company at VILKERATH and HOHKEPPEL. During the month the strength of the Battalion has been increased by 46 Officers, 1138 other ranks and decreased by 13 Officers, 296 other ranks. The Health of the Battalion has been moderate, average percentage of sickness 5½% (5"½). The weather has been generally warm and fine, with some snow at the beginning of the month, and rain towards the end.	

Robert Dunne
Captain & Adjutant
for
Lieut. Colonel.
Commanding.

2/4th. Battalion. The Queen's Regiment.

A.F. C.2118.

Reference maps:
Germany 3S. S.E.1/25000.
3L. 1/25,000.

WAR DIARY.

2/4th Bn. The QUEENS Regt.

PLACE.	DATE.	SUMMARY OF EVENTS AND INFORMATION.
EHRESHOVEN.	1.5.1919.	The Battalion was stationed in the EHRESHOVEN area from May 1st until May 28th 1919. During this period the Battalion was in Brigade reserve with one Company billeted in the factory buildings at BLISSENBACH (S. S4.), 2 Companies around LOOPE (S. 44.) and 1 Company at HOHKEPPEL and VILKERATH (S.04. & 13.). The whole of this period was devoted to training, which included firing on the rifle range.
	17.5.1919.	On May 17th 1919 Lieut.General Sir Aylmer Haldane K.C.B.,D.S.O. Commanding VI Corps inspected the Battalion in line and the billet areas (orders attached).
	26.5.1919.	On May 26th 1919 the 4 Companies moved into Camp near EHRESHOVEN (S.1-5-3-3-).
LINDLAR.	28.5.1919.	On May 28th 1919 the Battalion moved by march route to the LINDLAR area (copy of orders attached). In this area the Battalion finds administrative posts in the left sub-section of the Outpost zone, with one Company H.Q. at FRIELINGSDORF and one at HARTEGASSE and Bn.H.Q. and 2 Companies in reserve at LINDLAR (copy of defence scheme attached).
	May 1919.	Strength. During the month the strength of the Battalion has been decreased by 20 officers ....254 O.R. increased by 3 officers ....63 O.R.
		Health. The health of the Battalion has been good. Average percentage of sickness 3 %.
		Weather. The weather has been exceptionally fine and warm during the month of May.

The Corps Commander will inspect the Battalion in line tomorrow morning 17th inst. on the **football** ground EHRESHOVEN.

----

1. Parade will be as strong as possible. The following will not attend parade:- 2nd's in command of A & D Coys, Q.M.Staff, Orderly room staff, Medical and sanitary staff, Company cooks, 2 billet orderlies per Coy, 1 mess cook per Coy mess, 1 operator for each phone, 1 runner per Company.

2. Companies will be by platoons and not sized.

3. Dress:- Drill order.

4. Markers will report to R.S.M. on parade ground at 0945.

5. Companies to be on parade and in their places by 1000 hours

6. Os C.Coys will submit a return to B.H.Q. by 1900 today showing the strength of their Coy that will be on parade.. This return will also show those left off parade, and how employed.

7. O.C. H.Q.Coy will submit a return by 16.00 today to Companies showing N.C.Os and men on Headquarters that will be on parade. These will join their Companies on the parade ground.

8. Transport will not parade.

9. Officers will not be mounted nor carry sticks, and all N.C.Os will carry rifles.

10. After the inspection, the Corps Commander will inspect Company billets, cookhouses and latrines of A and D Coys at LOOPE at about 1040 hours. O.C Companies will pay special **attention** to all these places.

11. The 2nd in command of A Coy will be outside the school at LOOPE at 1040 and 2nd in command of D Coy outside Company Headquarters at 1040.

12. No working party will be found for the R.Es tomorrow.

                                                  (Signed) W.S.HOOKER. Major. for
                                                          Lieut. A/Adjt.,
16.5.1919.   2/4th Bn. The Queens Regt.

SECRET.

2/4th BATTALION THE QUEENS REGIMENT.

Order No. 2.

Copy No.....

27.5.1919.

1. The Battalion will relieve the 10th Bn.The Queens Regt. in the Outpost line in the LINDLAR sector tomorrow. 11th Bn.The Queens will take over the EHRESHOVEN area.
2. Advance parties of 1 N.C.O. and 2 men for each administrative post are being sent on this morning. Also suitable billeting parties from H.Q. and the 4 Companies.
3. The relief will take place as under:-
    A Coy 2/4th Queens relieve the right outpost Coy 10th Bn. Queens.
    B "   "   "   "   "   right support "   "   "   "
    C "   "   "   "   "   left support   "   "   "   "
    D "   "   "   "   "   left outpost   "   "   "   "
4. During the relief of each post an Officer of both incoming and outgoing Battalions will be present.
5. Arrangements for guides are being made between Os C. Coy's concerned.
6. The Battalion (less 1 pltn.B Coy.) will parade in mass on the football ground facing South ready to move off at 0830 tomorrow. Dress:- marching order. The Battalion will be drawn up from right to left as under:-
    C Coy - B Coy - A Coy - D Coy. and this will be the order of march with H.Q.Details leading. A distance of 100 yards will be maintained between Companies on the march.
7. The route taken will be the direct route across country, through the woods.
8. The transport will proceed by road via ENGELSKIRCHEN, marching off at 0830.
9. All defence schemes, plans for work contemplated and in hand, will be mutually handed over and taken over by all concerned.
10. All telephones and communications will be left in position.
11. All area stores will be handed over and taken over, and receipts will be given and taken for these.
12. The mobile reserve of S.A.A. and bombs will be exchanged.
13. 8 Lorries are reporting to Battalion Headquarters at 0800 tomorrow and these will be alloted as under:-
    1 to each Company at the camp area.
    4 for H.Q. and Q.M.Stores.
    All stores will be dumped ready for loading by 0745. Company stores will be dumped in separate stacks near the Guard room. All blankets will be rolled in bundles of 10 and clearly labelled.
    O.C. B Coy will detail an officer as baggage Officer to report to the Adjutant for orders at 1830 today.
    Each lorry when loaded will be accompanied by a man furnished with precise orders as to his destination.
14. The whole camp area and all billets will be left scrupulously clean and tidy.
15. O.C. B Coy will detail 1 platoon as rear party to complete the final clearing up of the Camp area. The Battalion sanitary staff and all available Pioneers will report to O.C. this platoon on the football ground at 0830 tomorrow.
16. Completion of relief will be reported at once to B.H.Q. by wire.
17. Acknowledge.

(Signed) P.COLIN DUNCAN.
Captain,
Adjutant,
2/4th Bn.The Queens Regt.

SECRET.

Copy No..........

DEFENCE SCHEME for the left Battalion (Lindlar Section)
Reference map 3 S. S.E.

---

1. The Battalion holds the left Bn sub-section of the front alloted to the 2nd London Brigade.
   The 10th Bn.The Queens Regt is on our right.
   The 52nd Royal Warwickshire Regt. 68th Bde, Southern Division is on our left.

2. The line of demarcation of the neutral zone follows the line of the inter communal boundary.

3. Boundaries.
   (A) Right boundary: S 80.77 - BURG (incl) (S 67) WUSTENHOF (S 36) (excl) - REHBACH (S 15) (excl).
   (B) Left boundary: The inter communal boundary.

   Organisation for defence.

4. The Battalion sub-section is divided into
   (a) The outpost zone - (all the ground east of the main line of resistance and West of the neutral zone)
   (b) The main line of resistance.

5. Within the outpost zone, two lines of resistance have been selected, known as:-
   (a) 1st outpost line of resistance (Blue line)
   (b) 2nd outpost line of resistance (Red line)
   These two lines of resistance vary with regard to their distance apart.
   On the right 4000 yards and on the left only 800 yards.
   They follow the undermentioned general lines:-
   (1) 1st outpost line of resistance (Blue line) E of HARDT (S 85) - E of ROMMERSBERG (S 76) - thence along the high ground (S.77.78) to HORPE (S.79) - HILL 310 (N 70) - HONNINGHAUSEN (N 51) - N of Ohr SULZE (N 41) - STEINBACH (N 21) - Ohr STEINBACH (N 22) - S of OMMERBORN (neutral zone)(N 22) - HEMBACH (N 02) - BUCHHOLZ (N 15).
   (2) 2nd outpost line of resistance (Red line) VORDERSTEINEL (S 44 23) - High ground E of LOOPE (S.44) - E of HOLZER Kpf (S 46) - VOSSBRUCH (S 48) - Hill 279 (S 39) - HOFFSTADT (N 30) - W of Ohr BREIDENBACH (N 20) - High ground S of KURTENBACH (N 21) - W of KURTENBACH (N 11) - E of DELLING (N 02).

6. The main line of resistance which consists of a line of mutually Supporting, localities with Machine guns in pill boxes guarding the principal approaches, the whole line being wired runs as follows:-
   LINDE (S 20) - STEINHAUS (S 02) - HOHKEPPEL (S 04) - VELLINGEN (S 05) BERG - (S 27) - KEMMERICH (S 28) - N & E of LINDE (S 09) - E of Unt BERSTE (M90) - thence the Division on our left continue from E & N of SULZE (M.80 M.70) - BREIBACH (M.50) - Unt KALSBACH (M 52) and thence Northwards.

7. The troops alloted to the defence of the Battalion sub-section are as follows:-

   1 Sec   18 pdrs (2 Guns)
   1/2 Sec.M.Gs (2 M.Gs)
   2/4th Bn.The Queens Regt.

8. The task of the Battalion is:-
   In the event of attack to delay the enemy for at least 24 hours in order to enable the Main line of resistance to be manned by other Troops of the Division.

   Action in case of alarm or attack.

   The following will be the procedure on receipt of orders:-
   (A) Move to position of readiness.
   (B) Man battle positions.

9. In the event of (A)
   (1) The Sec R.F.A. will occupy a position in observation at S 19.78.
   (2) The 1/2 Sec. M.Gs will take up a position on the N.W. slopes of Hill 279 (S 39).
   (3) The Companies now finding the administrative posts will withdraw to billets in rear of the 1st outpost line of resistance para 6(1) ready to man and fight on that line with their line of observation on or East of that line.

- 2 -

The dividing line between Companies will be:-
HONNINGHAUSEN N.33.97 (point where 2nd outpost line of resistance cuts the BRUCK (S 19). HARTGASSE (N 52) road) - thence down the R.SULZE (incl to left Coy).
(4) One platoon from the Company billeted in the school in LINDLAR will move to ALTENRATH (S 58).
(5) Two Companies (less one platoon (para 4)) will remain at LINDLAR.
(6) Battalion Headquarters will move to Orderly room LINDLAR.
(7) H.Q. of outpost companies will be established at VORD (N 60) and HELBACH (N 41) respectively.
(8) Ammunition of every man except No's 1 & 2 of Lewis Gunners will be brought up to 120 rounds. This ammunition will be issued from the Q.M.Stores.
(9) All surplus kit of outpost Companies will be collected and later conveyed to LINDLAR under Battalion arrangements, but if there is no time for this, it will be collected under Company or post arrangements (according to situation and time available) and principle inhabitant given to understand that village or house will be held responsible for same.

10. In the event of (B) either
(a) Steps enumerated in (A) will have to be taken or
(b) they will at once be taken with the following additions.
(1) Outpost Companies will at once take up their battle dispositions.
(2) The Company billeted in the N.W. end of LINDLAR will man the 2nd outpost line of resistance (Red line) from the SULZE RIVER (incl) - DELKING (excl)(M 92). Company Headquarters will be established at SPICH (N 10)
(3) The platoon at ALTENRATH (S 58) will detach one section to high ground in (S 67) South of BERG in order to keep touch with left post of 10th Queens at ROMMERSBERG (S 76). This platoon will also watch the country East of ALTENRATH and patrol towards HORPE.
(4) Battalion headquarters will remain at LINDLAR with a forward command post at junction of tracks S.53-04.
(5) Each Company will be made self supporting with:-
    1 Lewis gun limber.
    1 Limber wag. (S.A.A.)
    1 Cooker.
(6) Left front Company will send at least 2 men to the right front Company of the Battalion on our left at HEMBACH (N 02) to remain with the latter and act as liaison.
(7) Surplus kit stored at LINDLAR will be evacuated to LENNEFER (R 84).

11. <u>Action in case of atack.</u>
We must delay the enemy at least 24 hours.
(1) Front outpost Companies will hold their ground making every endeavour to keep touch with companies on their flanks.
(2) If forced to withdraw they will do so to the 2nd outpost line of resistance ~~where the Battalion will fight it out.~~ manoeuvering and fighting every inch of the ground.
(3) There will be no withdrawal from the 2nd outpost line of resistance where the Battalion will fight it out.
    Bn. report centre.....................FALKENHOF (S 38)
    Bn. forward command post..............N.W.slopes Hill 279(S39
    R.Outpost Coy report centre..LINDLAR.KEMMERICH (S 28) Road.
    L.   "   "   "   ..SPICH (N 10) LINDE(S 09) Road.
    3rd Company   "   "   ..SPICH (N 10) LINDE(S 09) Road.
    4th Company   "   "   As ordered.

12. <u>ACTION IN CASE OF CIVIL DISTURBANCES.</u>
1. Should civil disturbances on a large scale be apprehended the code word MOSELLE will be sent to Battalions. On receipt of this code word:-
    (i) All troops will be at one hours notice to move.
    (ii) All Officers will rejoin and remain with their Units.
2. When it appears that disturbances are imminent, the code word RHINE will be sent out.

- 3 -

3. All Units will be responsible for the protection of their own headquarters, telephone exchanges, communications, billets, stores, and horse lines.

4. (a) All Units are responsible for assisting to put down fires in their areas, in co-operation with the Local Fire Brigade, taking over the appliances if necessary.
(b) Units will reconnoitre the fire appliances in their area, and Officers and N.C.Os will be detailed to take charge of fire parties.

5. A supply of candles or lamps will be held in reserve in case the Electric lighting supply fails.

13.
INSTRUCTIONS AS TO THE EXERCISE OF CONTROL IN THE NEUTRAL ZONE.

1. All persons attempting to cross the boundary between occupied territory and neutral zone, except by the authorised control posts, will be fired upon, whether in occupied territory or not. If individuals are thereby killed or wounded in the neutral zone the British authorities have the right to enter the neutral zone and bring them into occupied territory.

2. (a) German troops forming the garrison of security in the neutral zone will wear yellow brassards.
(b) Other German troops are only allowed within 2 kilometres of the Western boundary of the neutral zone with the previous consent of the British authorities. This does not apply to REMSCHEID, which place they are permitted to enter if required to assist in keeping order.
(c) Local police will wear white brassards. They are allowed to be armed and to be within 2 kilometres of our outpost line in the execution of their duty.

3. British troops are not concerned with riots, strikes, or other disturbances that may take place in the neutral zone, except in so far as they effect the safety of our Troops. Any information that may be obtained as to occurences of this nature should however be forwarded at once to higher authorities.

4. With the exception noted in para 1 British troops are forbidden to cross the boundary line into the neutral zone without reference to the General Staff at G.H.Q.

To meet the case of firing taking place in the direction of our outpost line, or of the safety of our troops being endangered by any action, civil or Military, on the part of the Germans, authority to order troops to enter the neutral zone is delegated to Corps Commanders, who at their discretion may further delegate this authority to subordinate commanders not below the rank of Brigade Commanders. Except in cases of great emergency reference should however, first be made to General Headquarters

5. Any attempt on the part of the Germans to contravene the regulations is to be at once reported to G.H.Q.

(Signed) P. COLIN DUNCAN. Captain,
Adjutant, for Lieut Colonel,
Commanding, 2/4th The Queens Rgt.

DISTRIBUTION.

Copy No. 1 --- War diary.   Copy No. 6. Q.M.
       2 --- O.C. A Coy.   7. S.O.
       3 --- O.C. B Coy.   8. T.O.
       4 --- O.C. C Coy.   9. H.Q.2/Ldn.I.B.
       5 --- O.C. D Coy.   10. O.C.10th Queens
       Copy No. 11 --- O.C. 52nd Royal Warwicks.
            12 --- File.

A.F. C.2118.

WAR DIARY.

2/4th Bn. The QUEEN'S Regt.		Reference maps:—
PLACE.	DATE.	SUMMARY OF EVENTS AND INFORMATION.
LINDLAR.	1.6.1919. 30.6.1919.	During the whole month the Battalion has remained in the LINDLAR area, finding administrative posts as specified in the May Diary. Educational and Military training has been continued during the month. Full preparations were made for the advance of the Battalion into Germany in the event of the Germans not signing Peace, but the Peace Treaty was eventually signed on June 28th 1919. **HEALTH.** The health of the Battalion has been good. Average percentage of sickness:— 3% **STRENGTH.** During the past month, the strength of the Battalion has been decreased by 5 Officers, 42 O.R's and increased by 1 Officer, 32 O.R's **WEATHER.** The weather on the whole has been fine, with some rain towards the end of the month. Lieut.Colonel, Commanding, 2/4th Battalion The Queens Regiment.

NAMES OF OFFICERS LEAVING THE BATTALION DURING
MONTH OF JUNE.

```
Lieut.Colonel  S.T.WATSON.    D.S.O.
2/Lieut.       A.H.WHITE.
Captain & Q.M. G.SEARLE.      M.C.
2/Lieut.       P.B.MATTHEWS.
2/Lieut.       J.L.KIMBER.
```

NAMES OF OFFICERS JOINING THE BATTALION
DURING MONTH OF JUNE.

Lieut.Colonel G.B.WAUHOPE.   D.S.O.

HEADQUARTERS
2/4TH THE QUEENS RGT.
No. 1359
Date 1.7.19

Army Form C. 2118.

WAR DIARY
or
INTELLIGENCE SUMMARY.

2/4th THE QUEENS REGIMENT.

(Erase heading not required.)

Place	Date	Hour	Summary of Events and Information	Remarks and references to Appendices
LINDLAR	1.7.1919.		The Battalion was finding the administrative posts in the LINDLAR sector during the month with Battalion Headquarters at UNTER HEILIGENHOVEN, 1 Company at FRIELINGSDORF, 1 Company at HARTEGASSE, and 2 Companies in support in LINDLAR.	
	16.7.1919.		On 16.7.1918, the Battalion was relieved in the outpost line by 7th Battalion Middlesex Regt., and was concentrated at FRANKENFURST camp. In this area, training was continued.	
	31.7.1919.		On 31.7.1919, the Battalion took over the guards in the COLOGNE and KALK area from 11th Battalion the Queens Regiment.	
			STRENGTH. During the month, the strength of the Battalion has been decreased by 1 Officer, and 106 O.Rs. and increased by 1 Officer, and 27 O.Rs.	
			Changes in Officers:- Lieut. W.G.PHIPPS invalided to U.K. 7.7.1919. Lieut. E.V.SCRIVENER. Joined Bn. from 6th Bn.Queen's 1.7.19.	
			HEALTH. The health of the Battalion has been good. Average percentage of sickness 3%.	
			WEATHER. The weather has been generally bad, with much rain.	

Robt Duncan Captain

for Lieut.Colonel,
Commanding,
2/4th The Queens' Regt.

Army Form C. 2118.

43 2/4 RWS

WAR DIARY
or
INTELLIGENCE SUMMARY.
(Erase heading not required.)

Instructions regarding War Diaries and Intelligence Summaries are contained in F.S. Regs., Part II. and the Staff Manual respectively. Title pages will be prepared in manuscript.

Place	Date	Hour	Summary of Events and Information	Remarks and references to Appendices
Frankenforst.	1-8-19.		The Battalion was under canvas and providing all guards in the KALK and COLOGNE area.	
	2-8-19.		Guards were taken over from the Battalion by the 26th. Royal Fusiliers in order that practices could be carried out for the forthcoming review, by the Army Council. Educational and Military training continued together with practices for the Review.	
	18-8-19.		Selected Units and formations in the RHINE ARMY reviewed by the ARMY COUNCIL. Owing to the non arrival of transport the Battalion did not participate in the review.	
	25-8-19. to 30-8-19.		Teams were sent to the Divisional Rifle Meeting at EBRENFELD to represent the Battalion. They rejoined on 30-8-19.	
			The remainder of the month was spent in the usual training.	
			During the month the strength of the Battalion has been increased by 1 officer 5 o.R. and decreased by 6 officers and 56 other ranks.	
			CHANGES IN OFFICERS.	
			Joined B. Major S.W. Seaman. R.I. Rifles. Left B. Major E.C.B. Hull, D.S.O. To U.K.	
			Capt. R.H. Nugent. To 52nd.B. Sussex Rgt.	
			Lieut. W.P. Roberts. To 6th. Bn R.W.K. Rgt.	
			2/Lieut.P.E. Mather. To 9th.Bn E Surrey Rgt	
			2/Lieut.P.V. Bygott. Do.	
			2/Lieut.B.J. Burke. To. Chinese Labour Corps	
			HEALTH. The health of the Bn during the month has been good. Average percentage of sickness 2.50 %.	
			WEATHER. The weather has been generally fine with some wet intervals.	

Blandy
Lt.Col.
C.O. 2/4th Bn The Queen's (Royal West Surrey Regt.)

HEADQUARTERS
2/4TH THE QUEEN'S RGT.
No.
Date

War Diary.
2nd. London. L.T.M. By.

> 2ND LONDON BDE.
> LIGHT TRENCH
> MORTAR BATTERY
> No. TM/A/244.
> DATE 1.8.19.

The 2nd London Light Trench Mortar Battery was formed on May 5th 1919 under the command of Capt. W. C. Leslie Smith, The Oxfordshire & Buckinghamshire Light Infantry.

The personnel were drawn from the 3 Bns of "The Queen's" Regiment comprising the 2nd. London Infantry Brigade.

About a dozen of the personnel had seen service with Trench Mortar Batteries during active operations and about 10 more had also seen service. The remainder of the personnel were men who had been drafted to the 2nd London Inf Bde from Young Soldiers Bns in England.

On its formation the Battery was accommodated in the villages of OHL and GRUNSCHEID, West of Engelskirchen on the Cöln Road. Headquarters were established at GRUNSCHEID.

While at Engelskirchen the Battery successfully carried out various kinds of training and was well prepared to take its part in the projected advance of the Rhine Army.

On July 17th 1919 the Battery was relieved by the 1st London L.T.M. By and proceeded in lorries to the village of BRÜCK, 7 kilometres EAST of Cöln. Battery Headquarters being established at 903 Olpinerstrasse.

BRÜCK.
1.8.19.

LIEUT.
CAPT.
CMDG. 2nd LONDON L.T.M. BATTERY

Army Form C. 2118.

WAR DIARY
or
INTELLIGENCE SUMMARY.
(Erase heading not required.)

44 2/4 R[?]

Place	Date	Hour	Summary of Events and Information	Remarks and references to Appendices
HAUS FRANKENFORST.	1.9.19. 3.9.19.		The Battalion was encamped at HAUS FRANKENFORST. On September 3rd, 1919, the Battalion moved by lorry to the HENNEF area, Battalion Headquarters was situated in SCHLOSS ALLNER, and the administrative Control Posts were furnished by 2 Companies, one with Headquarters at BROL, and the other with Headquarters at EISCHEID, finding one platoon at INGERSAUL. One Company found all duties, and the fourth Company was free to carry out training.	
	24.9.19.		On September 24th 1919 the Battalion moved by March route to MICHAELSBERG Monastery, SIEGBURG. One Company remained at ALLNER finding the administrative posts, one Company found the duties in SIEGBURG, one Company was reduced to cadre, and one company was free for training. (Operation Orders attached)	
	STRENGTH.		During the past month the strength of the Battalion has been decreased by 3 Officers and 174 Other Ranks and increased by Nil. CHANGES IN OFFICERS - Demobilised. Captain G. D. Henderson, D.S.O., M.C. 2/Lieut. P.B. Robinson. Lieut. F.E.G.Stanford. To R.A.O.C.	
	HEALTH.		The health of the Battalion has been fairly good, Average sickness - 4%	
	WEATHER.		On the whole, good - with a cold spell at the end of the month.	

[Signature] Lieut.Colonel.
Commanding,
2/4th Battalion The Queen's Regiment.

HEADQUARTERS.
2/4TH THE QUEEN'S RGT.
No.
Date 30. 9. 19.

Secret.

2/4th. Battalion "The Queens" Regt.

OPERATION ORDER NO.

Copy No.
22-9-19

1. The Control Posts now maintained on the perimeter of that portion of the Occupied Area held by the London Division are being withdrawn to

2. The general line ALLNER - NEUNKIRCHEN - MARIALINDEN - ENGELSKIRCHEN - LINDAR - DELLING (exclusive).

2. The passes of all civilians passing through the control posts will be examined as here-tofore and efficient movable barriers will be placed in position across the roads at these points to prevent Vehicular traffic passing without permission of the Posts.

3. On the 24th. September the Battalion less "D" Company and 1 Platoon "C" Company will move to billets at the Monastery at Siegburg.
17th. Royal Fusiliers are establishing a Post on the road junction at Ingersaull. On this post being established the Ingersaull Post will be withdrawn.

4. O.C. "B" Company will arrange to take over all Guards at SIEGBURG at present found by the 10th. Queens.

5. "D" Company Headquarters will move to Schloss Allner on the 24th. September.

6. Completions of moves and reliefs will be reported at once to Battalion Headquarters.

7. All Government property other than stores which are to be taken when moving i.e. perminant cook houses, latrines, ablution places, bedsteads, sentry boxes, etc. will be handed over to the Local Burgomasters and receipts in triplicate obtained and forwarded to this Office.
Local Burgomasters are situated as under:-

```
BROL          --------  LAUTHAUSEN
KALDRUAN      --------  Local Gemeinde
SELIGENTHAL   --------     do.    do.
ALLNER        --------  Lauthausen
INGERSAULL    --------  Neunkirchen
BISCHEID      --------  Local Gemeinde
```

All area Stores at Ingersaull which are not taken over by the 17th. Royal Fusiliers, O.C. "A" Company will arrange to hand over to the Burgomaster in accordance with above.

8. Separate administrative orders (including disposal of tents and marquees and march orders will follow.

Robin Duncan
Captain
Adjutant
2/4th. Battalion "The Queens" Regt.

```
Copy No. 1   O.C. A Co.
      2   O.C. B Co.
      3   O.C. C Co.
      4   O.C. D Co.
      5   O.C.
      6   Second in Command
      7   Q.M.
      8   T.O.
      9   M.O.
     10   ..
     11   S.O.
     12   E.O.
     13   R.S.M.
     14   War Diary
     15   File
```

Secret.   2/4th. Battalion The Queen's Regiment   Copy No. 19

OPERATION ORDER NO. 2   23-9-19

1. All tents and marquees other than those which will be handed over by "A" Co. to 17th. Royal Fusiliers will be struck and dumped at the Q.M.Stores at the Monastery SIEGBURG.

2. Practice ammunition will be moved with the Battalion.

3. Receipts in triplicate for the stores handed over to the civil authorities must reach this office tomorrow without fail.

4. The baths and disinfester at Soligenthal will be left complete with personnel for the use of "D" Company.
Baths and disinfesters for the remainder of the Battalion at SIEGBURG are being arranged.

5. Transport.

The following transport will be available tomorrow.

(a) 9 Lorries report at INGERSAUL for the use of O.C. "A" Company at about 0900.
These lorries will be used for conveying all personnel baggage and tents of "A" Company to new area. On completion 7 of these will return immediately to Schloss ALLNER and will be available for moving Headquarters and Q.M.Stores baggage. The remaining 2 of the 9 will be despatched to "B" Company at SELIGENTHAL to move their stores and tents to SIEGBURG.

(b) One lorry to "D" Company at BROL at about 0900 to convey "D" Company baggage from BROL to ALLNER and subsequently "D" Company tents from BROL to SIEGBURG. On completion of this duty this lorry will report to the Quartermaster at ALLNER.

(c) 6 baggage wagons to "C" Company at KALDAUEN at 0900 to move their stores to the new area.

Transport (to be half loaded) will be available for the use of the Q.M. and will proceed by road at a time to be arranged by the Quartermaster with the Transport Sergt.
The Q.M. will give the necessary orders to the lorry drivers to make second journeys up to the number necessary to clear completely all the stores from ALLNER.
All Headquarters stores will be ready for loading by 1100 hours.

6. MARCH ORDERS.
"C" Company less two platoons will join "B" Company at KALDAUEN at 0930 hours tomorrow, and the whole column under the command of Captain A.E. Heatley M.C. will move off to SIEGBURG independently.
Headquarter details will proceed to the new area immediately after the midday meal.
DRESS. - MARCHING ORDER.

Copies to all recipients
of Operation Order No.1
plus Battalion H.Q.

Robin Dunlop
Captain
Adjutant
2/4th. Battalion "The Queens" Regiment.

War Diary

September 1919

2ND LONDON BDE. LIGHT TRENCH MORTAR BATTERY
No. X.101
DATE 1.10.19

Monday 1st	P.T & Rec. Trng. Drill & Musketry.
Tuesday 2nd	Battery moved from BRÜCK to MIELENFORST.
Wednesday 3rd	P.T. & Rec. Trng. Drill. L.T.M. Trng.
Thursday 4th	" " Musketry.
Friday 5th	Education
Saturday 6th	Interior Economy. Billet & Kit Inspections. Education.
Monday 8th	P.T. & Rec. Trng. Drill, Musketry, Lecture.
Tuesday 9th	Education.
Wednesday 10th	P.T. & Rec. Trng. Drill, L.T.M. Trng.
Thursday 11th	" " Musketry, Lecture.
Friday 12th	Education
Saturday 13th	P.T. & Rec. Trng. Interior Economy. Billet & Kit Inspections. Education.
Monday 15th	P.T & Rec Trng. L.T.M. work. Musketry. Lecture.
Tuesday 16th	Education.
Wednesday 17th	P.T. & Rec. Trng. L.T.M. training. Musketry.
Thursday 18th	" " Drill, Lecture.
Friday 19th	Education.
Saturday 20th	P.T. & Rec. Trng. Interior Economy. Billet & Kit Inspection. Education.
Monday 22nd	P.T. & Rec. Trng. L.T.M. Trng. Drill. Musketry.
Tuesday 23rd	Education.
Wednesday 24th	P.T. & Rec. Trng. Musketry. L.T.M. work.
Thursday 25th	" L.T.M. Trng, Musketry, Drill, Lecture.
Friday 26th	Education.
Saturday 27th	P.T. & Rec. Trng. Interior Economy. Billet & Kit Inspection, Education.
Monday 29th	P.T. & Rec. Trng, Drill. Musketry. L.T.M. Trng.
Tuesday 30th	Education.

.... CAPT.
CMDG. 2nd LONDON L.T.M. BATTERY

www.ingramcontent.com/pod-product-compliance
Lightning Source LLC
Chambersburg PA
CBHW081252170426
43191CB00037B/2134